PRAISE for *SOCIAL DANCE a book of ballroom poetry*

Boll's words glide across the page like choreography, taking readers on a journey that is at times just good fun, and at other times, intensely personal. Her poems are a refreshing reminder to all that words are a dance, relationships are a dance, and life itself is a dance.
—**Lauren Warnecke**, Dance Contributor to the Chicago Tribune

Moving to the steady throb of love and desire, Boll creates poems that remind us that intimacy and dance and love are about coming together even when we move apart.
—**Joy Ladin**, author of *Fireworks in the Graveyard*

Filled with intense, musical rhythms and daring sound-play, this book incites ecstasy and gives the reader the sense that she is dancing. Open your heart to… and lean into Boll's "delicious/ succulence and luscious licentiousness." You will not be disappointed!
—**Ann Tweedy**, author of *The Body's Alphabet*, 2017 Bisexual Book Award in poetry

Oh, how I love this exquisite volume of voluptuous, ecstatic poems! She opens the space of each page like the stage of a theatre where her poetry unfurls in a succession of lush and tender dances. She has invented a series of elegant compositional structures…that perfectly accommodates the eager rush and undulating sensuality of her language…
—**Peggy Baker**, dancer/choreographer, C.M., LL.D., D.Lit, O.Ont.

Social Dance evokes such joyfulness I had to call my partner over to try out the dance instructions that lie between poems. The poems…evoke the mystery of relationship, the longing too. There are also poems about her mother, understanding what is mother, what is herself, and an evolution into health… Hard-won truths beneath joyous poetry make for a fun, but vital, read.
—**Laura Foley**, author of *Joy Street and Night Ringing*

Only someone with a deep understanding of dance and the body and love can write a poem that repeats four words and leaves one breathless as "Terpsichore Two-Step (I love to foxtrot with you)" does—this is what it is to dance a poem. The poet asks, "Will you have some more?" and we kick off our shoes and say yes.
—**Flower Conroy**, 2017 Key West Poet Laureate and author of *The Awful Suicidal Swans* and *Escape to Nowhere*

Evoking the clever playfulness of a contemporized Gertrude Stein, the poems deliver "words of pleasure in endless / measure" and an energy that gets us up "doin' the two-step". *Social Dance* astonishes with ingenuity, grace and dazzling language.
—**Cora Siré**, author of *Behold Things Beautiful, The Other Oscar* and *Signs of Subversive Innocents*

This is a book in the space where the loops of poetry and dance overlap. It's a nice space to be, it shimmers…The poems are vocal, talkative, they're in a good mood. They're in love. O'Hara's "Personism" comes to mind...
—**Jack Hannan**, author of *The Poet is a Radio, Some frames: poems,* and *A Rhythm to Stand Beside*

Boll waltzes—sometimes with instruction, many times with questions, but always onward— Unafraid to say "I don't know"…*Social Dance* is a dedication to loving and a prayer for the eternal.
—**kathryn l. pringle**, author of *Obscenity for the Advancement of Poetry*

This book delivers more than a collection of poems; it's an invitation…in joyous leaps and measured steps…rendering a thoughtful glimpse into the inner and outer dances that bring meaning to human relationships.
—**E.F. Schraeder**, Ph.D., author of *The Hunger Tree*

One of my favorite questions to be asked when my wife and I are getting to know new people is "how did you two meet?" I love that question not so much because I love to tell the story, but because I delight in hearing which story each of us will tell at any given time. Carolyn Boll's *Social Dance* delights in that same way…a complex pas de deux that unwinds and rewinds a story of love's possibility becoming manifest.
—**Annie Bissett**, artist

The delightful illustrations of dance steps sprinkled throughout the book keep rhythm with the words that nimbly trot and skip…A joyful romp through life and love grounded in the hard work of devotion and commitment to that same love and life.
—**Holly Friesen**, artist/painter

Nuanced in its expressions of love and elegantly simple, *Social Dance* is a wonderfully paced play of words and image…Carolyn Boll will awaken in you the desire to dance cheek to cheek with your beloved.
—**Gabriel Dawe**, visual artist

Social Dance trips the light fantastic across the pages and pays homage to Love via poems that track its progression from courtship to "calm peace."…Boll demonstrates that Love is indeed a fancy dance that delivers "pleasure in endless measure."
—**Shelley A. Leedahl**, author of *The Moon Watched It All*; *I Wasn't Always Like This*; *Listen, Honey*; and *The House of the Easily Amused*

Full of joy and charm, Carolyn Boll's debut collection is a playful and exuberant celebration of love and courtship.
—**Christopher DiRaddo**, author of *The Geography of Pluto*

In Boll's deft hands, the varied rhythms of relationships are mirrored not only in the dance-step diagrams interspersed throughout but in her formal variation as well. And though these accomplished poems are light on their feet, they remain firmly rooted in the body with its enduring hungers.
—**Kristina Bicher**, author of *Just Now Alive*

These poems and images reflect a way of living that is intuitive but structured, heartfelt and thoughtful, and that recognizes the depth of balancing both joy and sorrow. *Social Dance* a book of ballroom poetry folds and unfolds into life…like an origami swan… leaving us soulfully satisfied with the piece we're holding in our hands.
—**Darla Johnson**, choreographer, poet, dance educator, and author of *The Art of Listening: Intuition & Improvisation in Choreography*

Social Dance

◄ A BOOK OF ►

ballroom poetry

Social Dance

A BOOK OF

ballroom poetry

BY
Carolyn Boll

Sally Jane Books
2017

To my beloved Sue

ISBN: 978-0-9987610-1-5

Cover & book design by Elize Bogossian | ebogossian@gmail.com

PUBLISHER

Headmistress Press / Sally Jane Books
60 Shipview Lane
Sequim, WA 98382
Telephone: 917-428-8312
Email: headmistresspress@gmail.com
Website: headmistresspress.blogspot.com

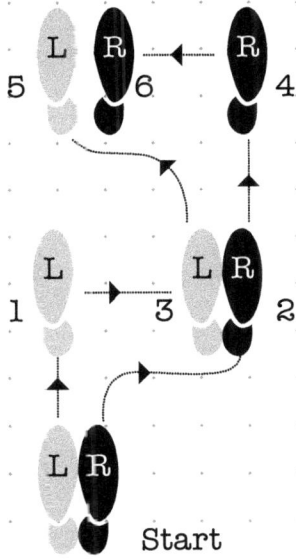

5 L R ◄······ R 4
      6

1 L ····► L R 2
        3

L R
Start

Who pulled who?

You ask

Who pulled who across
the kitchen table?
Who told who and when
with words or breath
or the choice of a
well loved leather jacket
that someone they
had met was
hopefully and full
of hope maybe
juicy maybe
their beloved?

So who pulled who across
the kitchen table?

Well I ask you

When did that pull
begin?
With a look
a knock at the door
an offering of tea
or brownie or
with
an interwoven
message through
star crossed threads
unravelling and

Was that who pulled who?

Was that who
began the wheels turning the pages
churning the locks opening?
Was that who pulled who
in such a way that you found
you and I found me and together we could begin
the leading and following
that brought we
to each?

Who was that who
pulled us together so that we
could reveal
the coming
attractions of infinite
variation and endless beginnings
asking really asking
a question

the real question

Me? Why me?

And so

drawing

nearer to you

I say

I don't know

You

tell

me

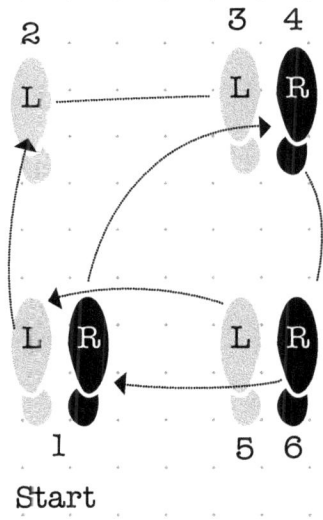

2   3 4

L   L R

L R   L R

1   5 6

Start

15

Come Out *to Dance*

perchance	*perchance* I wish for you	I wish for you
are you	*are you* sweet	sweet
the one	*the one* treasures	treasures
I've been	*I've been* I whisper to you	I whisper to you
dancing	*dancing* delight	delight
towards	*towards* I sigh across	I sigh across
all these	*all these* the room	the room
years	*years* and go	and go
spins	*spins* start	start
rhymes	*rhymes* become	become
and reason	*and reason* able	able
explored	*explored* at	at
endlessly	*endlessly* last	last
let's dance	*let's dance* to dance	to dance
and become	*and become* with	with
one	*one* you	you
no you are	*no you are* we	we
not the one	*not the one* lovers of	lovers of
we are	*we are* old	old

17

Beyond pas par pas

panic pas
step by step

so

go slow

beyond

no by no

two

yes by yes

Note:
pas, 1) French masc. n., step; *pas par pas*, **step by step**
2) French adv., not; *panic pas*, **panic not**

25

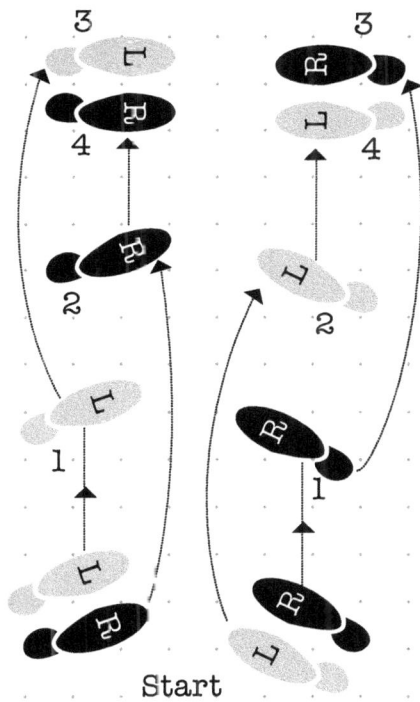

Start

Two becoming *one*

exhaling I become one	*exhaling I become one* O	O
taste me	*taste me* and so	and so
taste me fully	*taste me fully* as one	as one
and then	*and then* O	O
come	*come* pearl	pearl
to me	*to me* opalescent	opalescent
and be	*and be* curved	curved
unashamed	*unashamed* possibility	possibility
unprepared	*unprepared*	
and	*and* can we love	can we love
undressed	*undressed* and play	and play
cry	*cry* and	and
laugh	*laugh* dance	dance
yes	*yes*	
and embrace	*and embrace* yes	yes

gathering strength

gathering
strength
at the edge
of the world

somewhere
below the surface
pushing towards the unknown pulling back stronger still
an ancient voice

pools in the depths
a force
of possibility
and I begin to rise

unwinding
swirling ever higher
scooping
recoiling then up and above

the surface
now breaking through
the spiral unwound
the tip of the curl

suspended

above the past and
below the sky
the open sea behind me and looking forward
the shore

calling   and
release

rolling tumbling
undulating potent
sea
and sand

grains
come with me to the land

beyond eternal

I arrive rippling
and lapping
slowing
and tickling

this woman barefoot
looking out wondering about

where she has come from
and listening too

watching my mother

storm watch
out to sea
I watch
and see time and
the eternal

my watch
an eternity
now and
minute by minute
its blue face
round and
flat like
Columbus thought the
world was
and over the
edge you'd
go sweeping

through time

unable to
come back
lost at sea

tick
tock

was it
a matter
of time
mad like
she

tick
tock

not
me

I have

somewhere

to
be

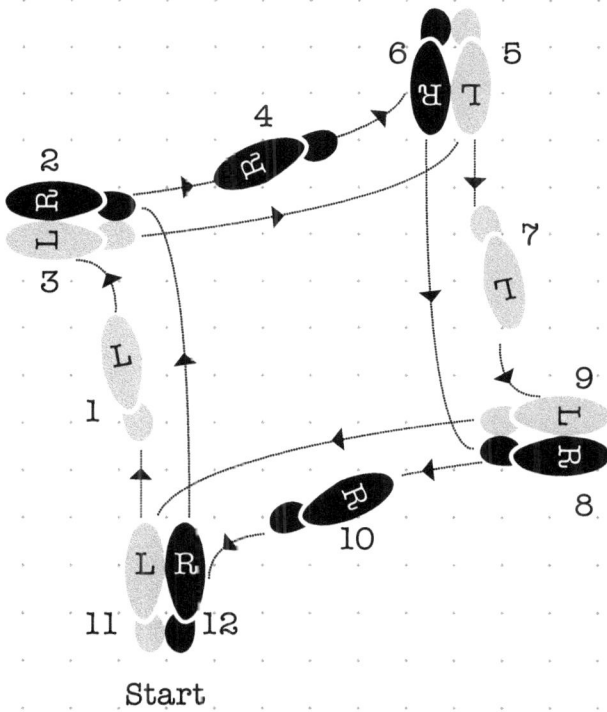

6   5

4

2

3

L

1

7

L

9

8

R

10

L R

11   12

Start

Love Pending

Love pending

                                   flying

                       time

whispers   stretching

                                                  out

across   eternity

                                a breastbone

                      cracks   open

                           heart

Your love is a tonic

Your love is a tonic
For what some people say
Is a disease uncomfortable
With life we slip and slide
Into unrest until the day comes
And comes and comes in cyclic
Abandon when the truth
Is revealed love is not a
Sickness but a well an endless
Elixir and licking you I have
Lapped up the health benefits
And feel fit to proclaim this
That this sweet madness
Is the cure not the ill

Will you have some more?

Yes please I believe I will
And will believe that
This is so forever

more

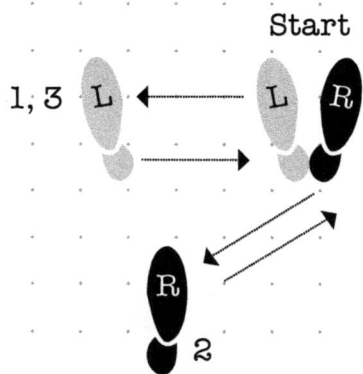

Start

1, 3 L ← L R

R

2

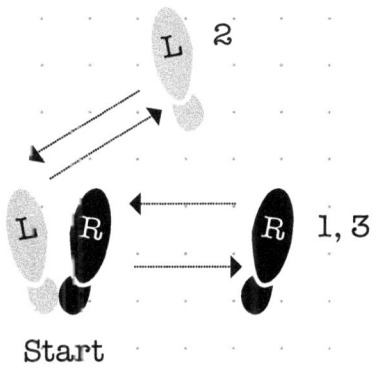

L 2

L R

R 1, 3

Start

41

Chemistry

compounded by the chemistry
of the moment
a little bit of this
and a little bit of that

and shaking it up
and throughout
comes
words of pleasure in endless

measure
again and again
your weight welcome
upon me your breathe
heavy in my ear
the sounds of
the waves

swirling and again and again
penetrating pondering
and pensive we

you and me

pretend not to look
though we both do and

cannot resist

laughing

in delight

The Big Questions

A dolmade darling?
ramen my ravishing?
martini or margarita?
sour cream and chives
or three cheese if you please?

Oh the decisions
  the choices
    the wants needs and desires
      of a day on vacation
        with my beloved

calm peace and the light of laughter
reign as our kingdom of love and delicious
succulence and luscious liscentiousness
leave us wholly
satisfied and
faced with

the real questions of life

breakfast my muffin?
curry my favoured one?
or ham yes ham
with maple syrup to
sweeten my days with you

And dessert?

No not tonight dear

Just you

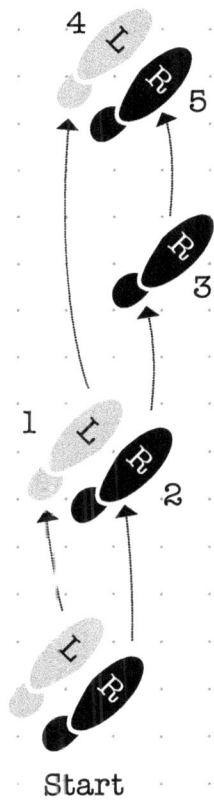

Start

45

Line dance

belovedyoubelovedmeconnectedalwaysyes

Sire

Sire
sigher
sigh
her...............

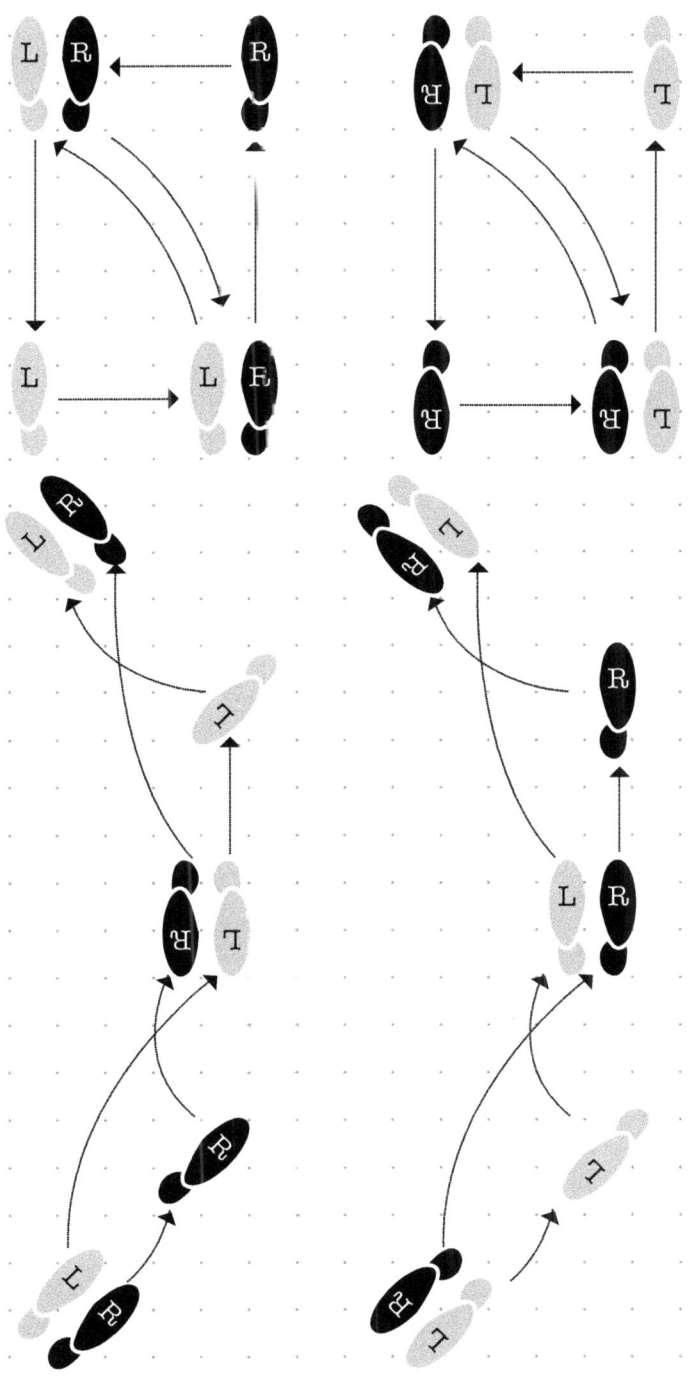

Salon de la Mariée

We're goin'
To the Salon de la Mariée
Goin' dancin'
At the Palais de congrès
Wedding marches
And hey what the
Hey -
Wedding cakes
And who's goin' to pay
No matter -
We've got
Two laissez-passers
Hmmm…band or DJ?
And what about the bouquet?

We're goin'
To the Salon de la Mariée
Goin' dancin'
At the Palais de congrès
What about waltzin'
Down the allée
With one another
All the way
Oh what to wear
On this special day
When doin' the two-step
And of course what to say -
To love, cherish
Honour

and obey?

We're goin'
To the Salon de la Mariée
Goin' dancin'
At the Palais de congrès
Nothing can
stop us
Hip hip
hooray
We're plannin'
Our own
special day
Shufflin' and steppin'
Get out
of our way –

We're goin'
To the Salon de la Mariée
Goin' dancin'
At the Palais de congrès

Note:
Salon de la Mariée **bridal show**
Palais de congrès **convention centre**
laissez-passers **free passes**
allée **aisle**

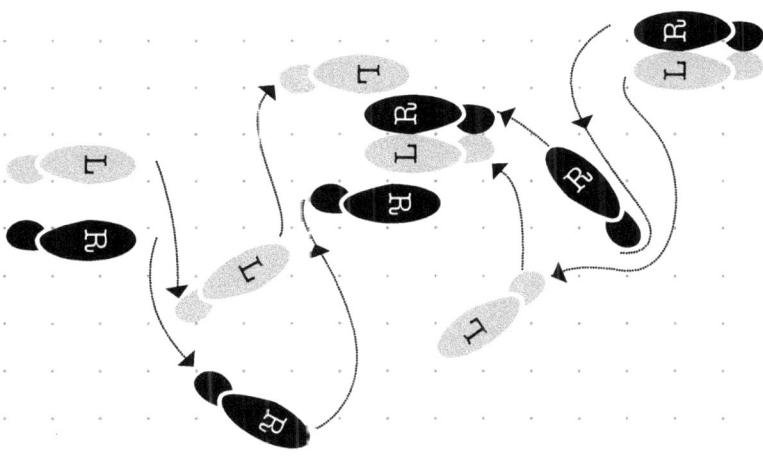

Terpsichore Two-step
(I love to foxtrot with you)

and

slow
slow
quick quick

slow
slow quick quick

slow and quick

slow slow
slower
slow

and

slower
slower

quick quick slow

slow slow

quick
      and slow
           and slow
              and slow

quick quick slow and   quick and   quick quick slow and
quick quick quick and slow and

slow and slow and slow and slow
and quick and slow and quick and quick and quick and slow and
quick and quick and

slow

                                 slow

slow

                                       and quick
                                     and slow

and

and quick and

slow

          slow
               slow and quick

and slow
slow slow slow and

quick and quick
and

slow
slow

slow and quick
and slow

slow
slow

quick quick

and

slow
slow
quick quick

slow

slow
and

slow slow

quick quick

slow
and

slow

and

Sweet Honey Husbandry

You sweet Sue
are truly the apple of my
no longer
roving eye

You sweet Sue
are truly the dance of my
life that has brought me
to you

You sweet Sue
are truly my mate my soul
my passage into
the beyond

You sweet Sue
are truly the honey
of my
hungry hand

for it is this hunger that set me
on this path towards you
and it is this hunger that
led me to know my own
appetite

and eating of the vine I
tasted testing for my truth
until that one drop told me
my truth was and is
you

Sweet honey husbandry
administering to our own home
and pleasure droplets of
dew and down and waking making
bread sweet breads or
herbal or spiced grains
of receptivity and reciprocity
an exchange and economy of
kisses

strokes and larder
femme and fodder
we compliment each other daily
upon our appearance
upon opening
our eyes

though in the night
we have travelled
together breathing our passages
open to far worlds

count me in count me in
we two a household embrace of rooms and mating

honey get the honey
so that I might lick you
one last time before tea

sweet honey husbandry
sitting down to talk
we still smell each others
appetite completed

complementing each other
as we sit down to talk
oh how we imagine this
nest castle honey combed
lattice might be

administered swallowed
drunk down from wee cups
tilted upwards our lips
telling all

You sweet Sue
and I dear me
agree to love honour
and feed each other
always with all the
best each of us has
to offer the other

You sweet Sue
and I dear me
will drink and flirt and
wait for our place at the mirror

dressing
to go out.

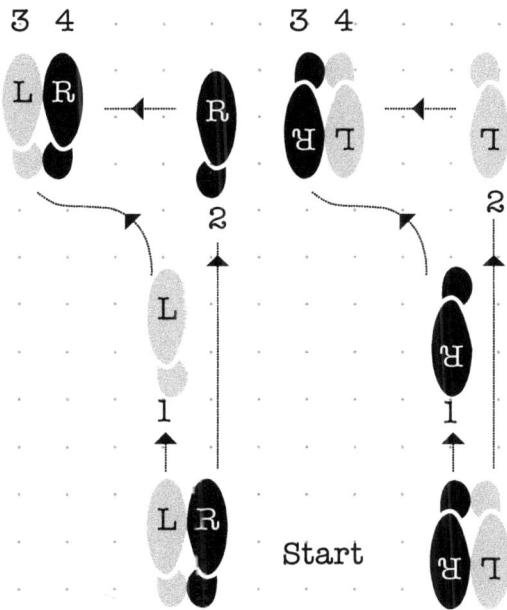

Acknowledgements

Thank you to The Gay & Lesbian Review and to Mary Meriam at Lavender Review for her early support of my work

Salon de la Mariée The Gay & Lesbian Review

Sweet Honey Husbandry Lavender Review

Terpsichore Two Step (I love to foxtrot with you) Lavender Review

Thank Yous

I want to thank Elize Bogossian, who created the cover and designed Social Dance. Her vast talent and her enthusiastic and spirited creative contribution at every step of the way, literally helped make my dreams come true.

And thank you from the bottom of my heart to Headmistress Press – and now Sally Jane Books as well. Co-founders Mary Meriam and Risa Denenberg are truly making the world a better place. Through their devotion to publishing and honouring lesbian voices, readers of all kinds, the world over, are discovering the depth, breadth, range and motion, that make up the many diverse and interconnected songs and dances of our lives. I am honoured to be part of this vital and vibrant movement.

Headmistress Press Books

Fireworks in the Graveyard - Joy Ladin

The Force of Gratitude - Janice Gould

Spine - Sarah Caulfield

Diatribe from the Library - Farrell Greenwald Brenner

Blind Girl Grunt - Constance Merritt

Acid and Tender - Jen Rouse

Beautiful Machinery - Wendy DeGroat

Odd Mercy - Gail Thomas

The Great Scissor Hunt - Jessica K. Hylton

A Bracelet of Honeybees - Lynn Strongin

Whirlwind @ Lesbos - Risa Denenberg

The Body's Alphabet - Ann Tweedy

First name Barbie last name Doll - Maureen Bocka

Heaven to Me - Abe Louise Young

Sticky - Carter Steinmann

Tiger Laughs When You Push - Ruth Lehrer

Night Ringing - Laura Foley

Paper Cranes - Dinah Dietrich

A Crown of Violets - Renée Vivien tr. Samantha Pious

On Loving a Saudi Girl - Carina Yun

The Burn Poems - Lynn Strongin

I Carry My Mother - Lesléa Newman

Distant Music - Joan Annsfire

The Awful Suicidal Swans - Flower Conroy

Joy Street - Laura Foley

Chiaroscuro Kisses - G.L. Morrison

The Lillian Trilogy - Mary Meriam

Lady of the Moon - Amy Lowell, Lillian Faderman, Mary Meriam

Irresistible Sonnets - ed. Mary Meriam

Lavender Review - ed. Mary Meriam

CAROLYN BOLL is a writer based in Montreal, Canada. Her poems have appeared in *The Gay & Lesbian Review* and *Lavender Review*, where she was the Guest Art Editor for the Dance Issue, and where she has had her collage work published as well. Her short story *Do You Know the Way* appeared in the LGBTQ issue of *Mayday Magazine*.

The recipient of Canada Council and Quebec choreography grants for early works that often explored the intermingling of dance, words, and projected images, Carolyn Boll has a BA in Western Civilization and Culture, and an MA in Media Studies from the research-creation option at Concordia University. She has attended writing retreats at the Fine Arts Work Center in Provincetown and is a graduate of the Humber School for Writers Post-Graduate Mentorship program.

A NOTE FROM THE DESIGNER ELIZE BOGOSSIAN

Inspired by Carolyn's poetry and her actual dreams, and the desire to help create an experience that takes the reader on a journey, I began with what I feel is the anchor of this love story: "Two becoming *one*." Choosing a Garamond serif-style typeface to enhance the timeless quality of the poems, I then used the play between regular text and *italics* on the cover and throughout. Movement and space were echoed in the brush strokes on the cover and with the dots on the pages with dance steps. I am grateful to be part of this collaboration – this marriage of words, images, music, and dance.